Songs for Sleep

Angela Yarad

First published in 2023
Copyright © Angela Yarad 2023

ISBN 978-0-6459342-1-2

Cover illustration and design by Angela Yarad

for the dreamers

Contents

Preface III

So, when the sounding drums of your heart
Thunder a score of change,
Know it is your love for the world
Which propels you to move

And you will do so
With such grace and strength
That the future will look to you in awe,
Through narrations of art and peace

I

I'm still trying to make sure
I fall in love with my whole self, first,
Not just the little parts of me
That make everybody else happy.

Let's Not Die on the Dining Room Table

How do I explain breathlessness to you?
Heavy fears incoming
Slow
But deeper, harder
Chest and stomach
Churning
Writhing and welling
Up to my eyes,
The body has been thus disturbed
There's nothing left to do but cry
And ease tensions.

The stability is there
Beneath you;

At the table
I let myself leak
Into the bowl,
As my family leaves me here
Disappointed once more
Tired of it all.

Just because you ask me how I am
Once or twice a year
Doesn't mean I'll be alright,
Doesn't mean I'm still not rocking
Myself slowly, blindly
Soothingly in the night.

In the suffocation:
Breathe

How do I explain breathlessness to you?
Onset by tiredness
Failings in support
It feels like drowning
A year of starving,
The internal mummification
Incompatible with its shell,
One day it bursts
Leaving trails of trauma
Before starting all over.

The abyss –
The voices of my past
The people shouting at me
I'm not enough,
Like the mosquitoes above my bed
I hear them taunting
Ensnaring all around
Out of and in my head,
Preying on me
Like vultures
On the carcasses of the undead
And I feel them drain the life from me –
Such is the stomach of my anxiety.

And you think I am weak
Because no one else has told you stories
Of how some people take their air
Differently to you,
And you don't believe it.

Even so,
I will not die here today

Holding myself up from the table
To move away from this side of existence.
Depleted, numb,
A solemn laugh into the mundane
Of the next daily task,
Nothing has really happened here, I swear.

I wish I could explain breathlessness to you.

Tonight, I lay
Vowing to make tomorrow great
With each inspiring notion
Motioning through me
Like thin creeks
Flowing to my ocean heart.
I am full
Of the moon's light

This morning, I forget
Last night's devotions,
I am loyal to the silk of my pillow
And the shame of my paralysis.
I've rested with the rain clouds too long

I'd like to climb into the sun
And let it furnace me for a while

Why can't my night owl body
In all its artistic glory
Live among the day people
And move like them?
I've fallen for light beams,
Streaming hope
So far from my reality,
It's almost easier never to reach for them.

P REDETERMINED R ESISTANCE

Clenching at strands of grass
For focus,
Boys gift stained daisies
And suggestive smiles

Under the library awning
Kissing her cheeks
And shaming her to give up
On dreams.
Teaching her to resist
Sharing love

Pity
Pity
Pity
Those who don't believe
In happiness.

She kept the rotten flowers
Without their rotten smirks
As a reminder.

And a reminder
Before she returns to those
Who held her hands on trampolines
And helped her to the sky:

Grow
Grow
Grow
Out of this space
Of social fears.
Thought she aged out of childhood
And boy giddiness,

Nervous practice talks
To the mirror

     How to make new friends
     And answer unnerving questions
     How to give herself without being herself
     How to hold back on affection

No, it's too much.
Shrink
Shrink
Shrink
Say nothing,
And the children go on laughing
Pretending they need nothing
And have nothing
To say.

Sad Girl in Graphite

Old carpet fraying
White with specks of dirt for colour
A fashion sense like vomit.
Smelt like filth
Of the sewer
Of the dirty man on the street who
You try hard not to show
How you hold your breath when you pass him,

The stranger you make no eye contact with
For fears of unleashing
Anger, provoked by your presence
Tainting innocent curiosity
Like the smoker with a bad brand
Polluting child lungs.

I cough at disgust
At the memory of the carpet I sat on
To play puzzles
In a room I mostly only saw
At Christmas, with a reluctant tree
And lights that outshone the happiness
Of the people who stayed there, and
Names on the baubles for children who were not loved.
The only pretty thing
Hung on the wall as art
A black and white of a sad girl, poor
To greet you at the entryway

Yes, the only real thing in the air was misery
Wafting through every crevice
Everywhere they went.
And they moved everywhere

The stench of death
Finding victims in new rentals
Every few years,
Along with the carpet and the sad girl
And the unwilling tree,
To host more scenes
Of the same genre;

Of children growing up too fast
Of rage
Of being looked at
Or touched
Or hung and shook,
Like the time
I played my puzzle
On the vomit carpet
And watched the women let things happen,
Before being dragged out for safety
Past the portrait of the sad girl
Welling up
Wishing me well, through the door
Leaving behind my childhood
And an unfinished puzzle.

SHADES OF BLUE

Mary never held me
I rocked myself
silently
never disturbing the women beside me.
I must breathe through whatever it is this anxiety
is trying to pull me away from

It will not consume me
though all signs point to my death,
The destruction of the soul
is the act of giving into the fear
and the shame of the emptiness the following day.

So often I believe I will be placed among those greats
who were glorified for what they could have been
whose internal traumas were too much to handle for more
    than a decade of trying.
But I don't want to run away like them
To a safe place they couldn't find before,

Like the arms of Mary
Great sheets glistening
to the holy celestial white noise
of the cloaking
made blue for its richness of symbolism.
Sway me
like the golden incense
beneath candlelit domes of silence
holding nothing but steady bell tolls and soft murmurs
Blinding iconography.
These people could not have been so real
as to have walked the soil I have walked

It is why I am so removed from them
and why these war times make it impossible for me to know
    them
to travel to their space
or simply past my own caging landscape.
I wish to remove the soul out of this body
to another more adaptable to the needs of a wanderer,

So as to not relinquish a great love
for the body's safety net –
the consistency of self-soothing
at the corner of my bed.
Anxious girl,
Stop robbing yourself the exploration of life
just because you think you're not good enough
You're the same as everybody else
blue with motherly melancholy,
I've never really known what you've been frightened of.

I Hate it When My Friends Talk Like This

I sit:
Stretching my face
Clawing at it,
Pounding fists against my body
My chest
My stomach,
Pulling tightly the tape from the bottom draw
Around my shapes, to mould them,
Surely one of these will work.
Then I check the numbers daily
Take the pictures daily
Nothing happens,
This skin is stuck to me
These bones shall never shrink
What a pity.

Tʜᴇ Hᴜᴍʙʟɪɴɢ

On the verge of confidence
My body began to fail me.
Should I be overwhelmed with gratitude
At the constant humbling?
People never see through the deceits of the mirror.

THE RUB

Ponders of the writer:
Memory or reality
Which in it is fulfilment
What is more poetic
Momentary happiness or the constant secondary
    exploration of it
Where are we more accessible in keeping love?

There's Nothing Else I Could Do

I am but an artist,
Not a real person,
Drifting specularly throughout life
Floating in a timeless space
Of other people's worlds,
Trying to find something to create from it.
These do not belong to me
I haven't lived these stories,
A mere observer
Seeing all its beauty,
Wanting to contribute a verse.

I hate labels.
I am nothing
I am everything,
I am always changing.
I am not the same thing I was five minutes ago
Minutes, days, decades,
Whatever time you go by
If time is a concept familiar to you.
I am nothing but the pulled strings
In a puppeteer's game.
I am nothing but the moving particles
Vibrating ever so close together
To make a shape
Visible to other shapes
Willed into life,
Interacting in this made-up place.
What a concept;
I am nothing
I am everything
I am nothing.

THERE ARE PROSPECTS OUT OF THE SHADOWS

You must dispel the steel covers of confinement
Wrapping your bed in hesitation
These fiends which mark your mind
Can be relieved with the breath of day
If you let it.

II

There is a light that shines beyond the horizon
        Never quite parallel to the moon,
Though simplicity would lead you to believe it

There is a growling beneath the dirt
Heard in between moments of silence,
Hot rocks bubbling
Soil growing
Giving
Sheltering
        Plants and ants and bodies,
This we know

A comfort.

There is a study
On civilizations
On groups of animals
On science fiction, mythology
On ancient texts
    A gift of greater thought:
An idea.

There is a thought
Of robotic numbness
Of acceptance
Of belonging in purpose
Of fairytales on importance
Of attributing a higher meaning to the combinations
    of atoms, more than the simplistic pleasure blend
    of time, evolution, and coincidence

There are many concepts
That wealth lives beyond the wheat field
That mysticism lives beyond the northern star
That plenty lives beyond the smile,

Such ideas

Led men to wars
Led men to hate
Discriminate
Enslave
Segregate
          Affiliate their minds with the torment of the unknown

Some things cannot be known.

Let us sit and tell stories of what we imagine to be real
Let us sit and sing songs to comfort the unrest
To ease the chest in its longing for content,
          For a moment let's forget the curse of the thought.

Tell me a story
Of the stars
Of the dreaming
Of the chosen people
Of nirvana
Of the son
Of the last messenger
Of the earth mother
Of darwin
          And see what studies can come from Venn diagrams,
As we contemplate the possibilities
Of the spirits shouting around us, or not

Of the ancestors laughing at our plans, or not
Of the ether circulating our destiny, or not
Of the species' continual misunderstandings in bias
    communication, or not.

There lies the comfort of inevitability:

That the only truth is in the belly of the fabrications we birth to
    fill our needs,
        That tomorrow we shall die and contemplation will be
    for nothing
But dissatisfying philosophy
And passing the rolling time –

Yet, another concept.

War Horse, Great (Useless) Rider

Sail my ode to the old friends
I only hear from in dreams,
May this homily arrive at the feet
Of boys living beneath the wheat.

I recall the drums and slaves to rhythm
Their mind battering for escape,
Tempestuous fears soaring
Across the rising gale
And rocking rickety guts,
Praying something of this life will prevail

There is bravery in the blind man
Led by generals, searching for intuition.

Sanctity in the remaining seas
Carrying bits of wood and metal,
Broken bodies to some shore;
No silence greater than the whistling winds
On the backs of dying dogs

Deliver them gifts of glory
Scripture, paper songs
About doing it for the same gods
Who spectate our earthly arena,
And chew on all those young men, out of eternal boredom.

Zenith

O sea
My heavenly beauty,
I hear you shuffle me to sleep
Across the road from my bed
Wantonly
Romantically
Pretending
As though you didn't almost drown me
Hours ago.

I thought you loved me
And I adored you.
My soul would mend itself in you
Your salt caressing
Softening my skin,
Your weeds flowing along me
Like I was their mother
Letting them pass over connected and free.

I deliberated being buried in you
Resting with you
But you want me too soon.
Don't scare me away
I'm not ready yet,
Don't tire me in your play
Seducing me in your rips
Pulling me astray
So you can have me to yourself,
I belong to other things too.
My doting child
I'm coming soon,

For now,
Unwrap me and let me lay
Melodically,
I know we love to wrestle
And you bring my youth to me
Just don't tumble me to the shore
I don't think I can do it anymore.

And yet
As I write this at 1:30 in the morning
I hear you
Beckoning
In your hushing over me,
Thinking of how I might dip into you
Tomorrow
And do some light reading.

In Short, Pleasure

Melancholia is the girl who does not age,
almost as solemn as the rose bud's wilt.

La Dolce Vita
Anita, dancing
in all her laissez-faire feminine instabilities
innocently luring him to taste the fruit of the gods,
the splashing of holy water.

If she were to sing lullabies to the echo within a city under stars
he would hear only the siren's invitation

When a woman is beautiful,
her goodness becomes godly
and her generosity, sensuality

Voluptuousness is man's language for transcendence -
currency they all long to revel in.

Shall the Fontana di Trevi
levy
purity for nature's ecstasy?
Is exuberance not all of these things,
nor sanctity in the stone statues she plays with?

We must come from all of this.
Sacred is the breeding ground of every urge,
sipping from intoxicating experiences
bonding soul to the fleeting now.
Each child's attempt to grasp it - a vision,
a curse

She may be calling to him
but she is reaching for life.

CHAIN WHISPERS

My women who have travelled great seas
And sown seeds
Whipped by the back on their knees
In a dark room in the night
Where they can't even cry
For the unwanted pregnancies
Please
Speak to me.

My women
Who have marched in the sunsets
Who believe in the glory that this too shall end
Swaddled babes strapped to their chests
Weaving baskets and banners
While the world is in bed
So the future may carry more bread
And choices
Speak to me.

My women
Whom with little have strived
Worked with less and survived
Against conformity, found might
Separated by segregation
While all at once still trying to fight
For a voice in your home, in your life
You're tired
Speak to me.

My women who hunger for change
For a world that only knows you by the name
You gave yourself

To demoralise fame
But stand for the hope of rain
Returning after all these heat waves
You will not starve in silence
All for everything to stay the same
On this land built upon by suits of pain
Thus I channel you
Speak to me.

The Difference in Men

It was party season
And we were leaving
Single file.
You, leading
Instinctively held my hand
Gently weaving fingers
So I wouldn't get lost in the sea
Of intoxicated dancers.
He, smiling
With such smug ownership
Grabbed me from behind
Before my sharp slap of shame,
That not one person
In this ocean
Witnessed.
And in that second
I saw,
Never have I felt so strong
The presence
Of the difference in men.

Therapy at 11:20pm

Young one
Of enigmatic air,
I found you swimming
And laughing
Before anything had really hurt you

Though you had been touched
An outcast in childhood,
Hope remained in your impurity.

Envy eyes watched you
Without knowing you;
Blind people
Think beauty solves everything

Men wish you were their merry-go-round;
You comfort their needs for flattery
Hoping they keep their promises of adoration,
All for the upper hand in your loneliness.

On the brink of adulthood
Your mother left you wary and red
To dig your own way
Out of the emptiness
Of your deep blue sea,

And in your paranoia
You wonder
Where have all the true friends gone?
But I see you,
Shining
Dancing like a God
As this moment frees you from the rest,

And I know you know
Somehow
You will make it to the end.

THE SEVENTH VEIL

They cannot make anything out of you
Which was not already there,
No structured marble
Chiselled to a David,
No glass frame
Or fine china to be displayed.
This daily pouring out of wasted energy
Of wasted life,
Which would be better used in something holier to your spirit,
May empty you
May kill you
But you will not die.
And if finally the moment comes
Where there be nothing left in you
Start again.

Remove this seventh veil
Find the nakedness of life
The simplicity of birth
Universally felt;
Perhaps the only equaliser.
The sidewalks of your city will not desert you,
Not the autumn leaves
Or the skyscraper trees
Nor the loneliness of these streets.
If there be nothing left in you
Return here
And start again.

Perfection does not exist
And it was never bred in you;

Quit this constant seeking
Ploughing of your soul,
You cannot weed it out.
But go into a field of flowers
Tasting only earth for nutrients
Only flora for sustenance
And there, the glimmer of it lives,
A home in the valley
The lake between hills
Bordered by moss and isolation.
Waiting for you,
When there be nothing left in you
Calling to you, to start again.

dear people / dear lovers and stars and skies / dear earth and oceans and friends / dear whatever idea of spirit you've been embedded into, dear god / dear people / we assume the thoughts in our mind can reach external understanding / if, in likelihood, they don't / hear this / let me dare insert my mothering on you / use me like a fountain, overflowing / drink from me and live / call to me in your years of separation and I will receive you / I won't think twice / empty onto me, my darling / I have too much love to sit with / and I refuse to inherit the wind // I want to be heard clearly / in the gentleness of my introverted family, we can smile across the table and know we are wanted / but do they know they are craved by me / when I write to my father's father, my faultless sweetheart, does he comprehend my adorations to the true extent in which they are intended / and in the silences of my social grandmother, when she grips to my hands and wraps herself through me, does she know she is allowing my heart to move in its natural order / I am full / and in disbelief that they truly grasp this / should they be my great happiness / I am content / but must accept that I shall die when they do // in the meantime, with this love, I can feed the world / my friends / will these words mean anything to you / are they understood / perhaps only in your return to isolation, your return to needing something / I will not abandon you / even if I've been abandoned / do you hear my songs / muted or not, they are playing / ringing out to bask in your joys / to weep in your trials / this is not shameful / this is true love / would it be the reality of the world / that a love which was, may not always be / rid yourself of this fear and stay by me / I may also be hurt, but I am listening / are you //

CRAVINGS

I will be the finger tracing the outline of your face
The eyes which adoringly hold your soul
The hug which extracts all pain,
I will be the fire which melts your walls of fear
And the boat giving you safe landing
To the shore of your dreams.
I will give you my ears and my heart of empathy
My hands which unveil all vulnerabilities
As they float over your body,
I will pluck all harmful stories
And replace them with kisses
Feeding you all the comforts you've ever craved.
I will give you all that I am
Sending out all that I want of another
Without ever expecting a return on my post,
I will be in your brief touches of tenderness
Chipping away at your stone walls
And maybe if I'm lucky
You'll remember me when I'm gone.

III

in the winter / nursing, burping, changing / soft singing / push bikes across the street / inside cafes, milkshakes / along the water, round the bend / the boys run away, she catches them / potatoes and pasta / the same shows, games played over and over and over / and tears / the boys say *i miss you* // in the summer / down the dunes / on the sand, in the floats / in the boat, on the crashing sea / the boys copy curses of fear and turn them into laughter / they hold on tight for life / in the apartment, under the table, behind the door, in the cupboard / hiding, giggling, ready or not / in the park, down the road / up the tree to rest / chasing and tipping on the grass / out of breath, they catch her / and the boys say *i love you* //

To Have a Sister

This moment:
An hour before midnight
Fruit drinks in the black car
After exercise,
My sister tells me about all the dumb shit she's done
And we laugh.
Or alternatively:
An hour or two after midday
Iced coffees in the white car
After exercise,
My sister tells me about all the dumb shit you've said
And we laugh.

These moments of freedom
I find, are fleeting.
Our youth stained within the seats,
Stories of out trials
Hum alongside the radio
When we're not screaming the tunes we know will later
    soundtrack these years.

And in this moment
I am nostalgic.
Fearful of the future
When we'll be reminiscent
Of these parked talks
Directionless drives,
Clearing our childhood
Mapping our future
And gossiping about the dumb boys who've drifted through
    our lives.

Brother,

My love,
you wrote me a letter, language you thought
I would understand: poetry. When did
the tables turn and you came to be proud
of me? How, in your determinedness are
you now my beacon of constancy?

When you rest your eyes, the sun also lays
with the clouds in reflection, concerned not
with the span of her rays. You will reach what
you will. My buds follow you forever.

When you were soft of eyes and tender words
I cried for you, that your bubble body
sheltered mine in its fragility. How
sweet to witness this. Now your tower shadows
me. Even in your fierce adoptions, there
still lingers gentility; streaming colours.

I miss my baby. Like my heart was ripped
from me, living wherever you are.
Growing, you have turned into this green light,
some understanding guardian angel
born to me, to teach and love and pester.
You were always mine, and you knew it. Now,
in your absence, you ring out to me, that
I may hang upon your every joke. You
tear me up. How did it all string along
so fast? There should have been iron lamp posts
signalling what were to be our simple days.

In our childhood, not too long ago, I
watched you in your bassinet, fluttering
in and out of consciousness. Now, traveller,
chaser of dreams, I watch you flutter in
and out of our home. Please return soon,
my love.

CAPRICORN

My mother is a mountain.
She watches peacefully
the streams at her feet
bubbling over rocks and the animals which feed from her,
the spanning trees
stretching from the base of her skin.
In their productions, erosions, and migrations,
she grows
but cannot move with them,
she is comfortable in the distance
in the disconnect.

My mother is a mountain
I slide down,
grasping at any shrubbery my
craving fingers find,
weeds
she refuses to release

I want to pull her to me
and hold on as long as I can
I want her to let me burr a hole through her body
so that I may set up camp and sleep there
I want her to need something from me,

She doesn't know
she does.

I can bind her to reality
she drifts too far for sanity.
Delusions seem optimal
for survival,

she talks to God and smiles
sitting on the other side of depression,
one step away from enlightenment

She talks of grey matter
she's satisfied, out of fear,
her repressed memories
find me in my dreams
I am haunted
so that she may be weightless.

I imagine
if I shrunk her to size
and laid her out on a couch
to unravel her time warped mind,
she would bend to me
and I could save her
finally.

There is peace in gravity.

My mother is a mountain
a boulder of strength.
If I died, she would be unmoved
she told me,
and maybe I want to hurt her for it.

So, I tend to her
pluck
prune
pull her thoughts apart and
play with possibilities of her psyche

so she may crumble;
a landslide of awakening

She would be broken
but she would love me.

And yet my mother is a mountain
and a summit is just a cliff.

And a Contrast

Like that song
Katie,
I love you,
I said, though I knew you were sleeping

maybe I'm the one who's lost

We are both beautifully broken;
Regret nothing,
In the rare moments when you ask me what went wrong
And we're all real for a while –
like years ago on hot afternoon drives
when I'd ask you about pain
and heard only truth –
it's good

So, Katie,
I don't know how else to love you,
or anyone else,
without honesty.

Tell me you love me,
I can't remember what it sounds like

foreign

Every time you touch me
I try not to cry

desperation

You're quiet and scared and beautiful
But, Katie,
this is it,
this may be the best it will ever be
Are you happy with me?

I hate that I love you so much

and I hate that I only find the time to say these things as you
    sleep.

Well, Katie,
Just wondering
I know you can't hear me, but
I love you, do you miss me?

Playing Word Association with the Olfactory
Bulb

The smell of your beer breath is hypnotic to me.
I can see my father as the sun eagerly sets
walking me through falling brown leaves
by Bourke St,
in a sweater and leather jacket.
I used to only follow him so he wouldn't be alone,
now I follow him for the echo sound of men
the intoxicating haze
of yeasty alcohol-stained shoes
spillage and fumbling
across cold wet grass

it's a pulse,
boredom made comfortable
because your daddy keeps you warm
and he's happy.

In a rare midnight talk
he said
I never want you to be with someone like me
and it broke my heart.
Because I've learnt to love people like him:
A duality of open-heart sensitivity
sealed away and locked forever in a
disciplinary stature of untouchability.
All anyone wants to do is reach inside his mind and find
what songs are being sung

or where he retreats to, when time slows down
and he comes to grips with his reality
when the distractions of the field have ceased.
Maybe I can find my father
over a decade ago
when we'd park
somewhere along the Marine Pde
at 6 in the morning to go summer swimming
and he'd teach me how to catch a wave.
I wonder if he thinks of me
when he's got nothing to do,
like he used to.

Four and Seventy

He sits at the desk with cards by the bed
of dusty naps below stills of a family
I don't belong to. I belong to no one but him.

He slumps on the couch. The sleeping babe
with a gold chain, in a wife beater.
He is no wife beater. But life is a cheater and
the ones you know may not be
who you know.

Everyone has disappointed me.

So, he does not answer the questions which may
disappoint me.
And I know he was not the person I know now.
But he is. Just as I will always be
this way.

Nobody has ever known me in the way he seems to
know me
as he holds my hand
in the only home he's ever owned. And he says to me,
my love, we are dreamers who will change the world together.

And it is not for money, which we'll never have,
and not for acknowledgement, for we know we'll never
be known. Lovers
of nature, trapped
in slow bodies, cursed
with suffering minds, disappointing
everybody who doesn't speak our language,

just so we can try to reach
the people
who do.

Thinking we are safe to love again
in people who disappoint us.
May we always be alone for it.

But please, I whisper to the wind
hoping it finds him,
don't leave me before
I find another soul like yours,
And he calls back
soft and soothing, *my love, my dreamer,*
we are of the same soul. We need not speak
to hear the words we long to say.
Our eyes need not lock
to feel the depths of our twin's emotions.
And so you already know
if time will let me go, I'll go,
it's been too long.
Then you will take
my strength and my words and be whole,
and so, never alone.

So, soon in my wandering
for belonging
I surrender to reality,
Repeating the calming
words of my histories. Spoken
by the only person to ever know me
though he may have never really known me.

Just as I
may have glorified the person I thought he
to be
because he belongs to me, though he may
never belong
to me.

I Have Your Blank Postcard

I have been missing you, Nonna.
Like you've been leaving me little notes
With your scent,
Lots of people do that to me
Haunting me with their love
Like they're calling me from afar,
Reminding me I still have them
Some place tucked away.
I have been dreaming of you, Nonna.
Of your eyes and of your skin and of your voice
Deep and giggly,
You were always young to me
Loving all the children,
Taking them all in your arms if you could
Sheltering them from the rain
With your sun for a soul.
I have been missing you, Nonna.

Easy Living

I know a love
With emerald rings
And porcelain things
Hounding on the love of duty.
I follow her chipped nail polish
Along parsley-stained wedding china
To the sounds of the cathedral radio,
Her stories of yesterday,
And opinion.

I hear
She is remembered
Wherever she's been.
And where she's been:
Brown drumming mountains
Like thunder from the body,
The cedar children
Dancing through war.

And though she's made her home
Nonchalant assimilation
In green mansions,
It was not always such easy living.
She forgets not the land
From whence she came,
Sitting in the holy music,
It lingers on her tongue
And in the skin of her love
Who she serves
Willingly, affectionately.

And he,
Curtaining her
In his name
The living legend of romanticism
And private spoils,
Spoils me
And his girl, hopelessly.
He calls her *angel, darling* –
Words I've known before;
And I want it.

And from all this
I've had my living
In the ease of such love,
They'll never know how I love them.

RICHARD

Stewart Granger, swashbuckling type
when I see you, I see heaven

Coffee and orchards by the morning sun,
I don't know where you belong
I whisper your name and cry
at the tune of it;
Time goes by.
Sun setting behind cypress through the kitchen window,
I don't know who you are
but I know you
as a bird knows a song
as a strong wind knows a whistle.

Some stranger, seen in running picture:
Tanned feet dipping
knee deep
beneath the black lake,
you hold me.
I create grained images of you from your chronicles
I want to bury myself in these memories
and see if you were ever like me:
Afraid of anything
in love with everything
in reach of something.

James Stewart, lyrical type
you share me with no one

My grip flowing back and forth
from your back to your shoulder,
almost cheek to cheek

spinning and bopping
with intermittent singing
to 'Valerie' of all things,
and I am in love.
You braid my hair intimately
I paint your eyes blue
and bend to your yarns and trials,
animated
as though they were of the good book itself,
gold plated and magnetic.

Does my sensitivity disarm you?
Many of these romantic notions were born of you.
When you held me in your arms
did you have dreams of this,
of who I would become?
To think you had me softly tended,
I have not changed

Would you wish that I were
different?

Stewart Granger, swashbuckling type
you are of my dreams

Through the clouds which swarm confusion,
warm me with melting light,
I am but a pool
to your structured stance.
Scoop me up and save me
with incandescence,

I belong nowhere farther than the eyeshot
of your smile
of your wink

But you know this,
Nothing could tear me from you.

IV

INTERLUDE

Shivering trees
Scraping symphonies at the windows,
Enduring long winter nights.
Whispers of tyres running the roads
Soft in the distance,
Growing with the pendulum.
Train line rattles
And their old whistles,
Now they honk.
Sinking into love,
Cautious love
Like rain sifting through soil.
Tin roofs
Dances of reverie;
Sounds to fall asleep to.

THE AFFAIR

Suppress the pain of remembering
Making movies with our dance,
Hugging each other
Tightly
Like it's the last time we would ever kiss
Goodbye
Beneath the lines at Central Station

Liquor fuelled yelling
And running
Before the bathroom door
Locking
On the homeless, sleeping
By the tunnels, in my home
Beneath the lines at Central Station

Deep yellow lights
The old knocking
Clock
And the echoed youthful singing
Every weekend night,
Breathing life
Beneath the lines at Central Station

These are not wasted years
Filled with touch and warm nights
Of an orange moon and black sky,
Whisper gently in my ear
One more time
Beneath the lines at Central Station

A Heartache Muse Came to Visit Me

You are painted across every emotion
I have ever known,
Spanning out shards of colour
In the setting hues of a melting indigo sky.
When nostalgia breaks
It is your body which brings my return;
Lightning, your passionate rage
I rain to cool your burnt land of love.

I spoke too softly for you to hear,
Yet not soft enough
For things to mean what I wanted them to.
In the vast turquoise sea
Where I see my grave,
Bound to the only things I spoke through:
Instruments which weren't enough to translate to you;
I lied if I seemed cool swimming in your foreign pools.

I sculpted my heart on letters
Initialling trees,
Breadcrumbs of my soul
Scattered perfectly randomly,
For you to find fingerprints of my scent
Pasted around your forestscape.
But you've lit the bark for ash
To repaint your greens and greys,
Evidence lost to the flames
Now there's nothing left of me
For you,
You blind, blind fool.

Sanctuary

My baby, honey
Dressed in white
lace and sheer pants
Closed eyes to the sky
Alive
In the garden.

My baby, darling
Wanting light
to be seen
Only wakes in the night
searching for his club Queen
Listening
waiting for her whispering
answered prayers
Except for Sundays
and their sunbeams
When he lays in my garden.

My baby, sweets
Gentle
as a floating lei
on calm waters
Seeming so far away
until my call
And he looks at me
briefly
before returning
to his search for identity
Drifting off
into nature
Mid-afternoon in our garden.

WHILE THE LAND BURNS SLOWLY

Old music hums
Waxing poetic
From behind French doors
And perfumes
Of the estate;
Life is full in the valley.

Pink champagne
And lemonade
In gold trim crystal coupe
By the pool and patio umbrella,
Watermelon juice droplets on the pavement.
Say yes to the scents of summer,
A heat which drives you to devour.

I rest at this ranch on the hills
Because the man who doesn't love me
Loves it here,
Wild stallion,
May he see me in these stills
And remember secretly we are the same:
Bedbound, sick of ourselves,
I don't want to end up like me.

'70s orange lounge
On the lawn
Musky and hazed like our memories,
It's been years
Of pretending
Not to notice he's gently preying,
But who's counting?

Colognes of ash and the green sea
Drift onto me,
Fingers stained with mint
Long after the meal
Taste the residue from underneath
My clear Hayworth filed nails.

Remember not to love him
But to let him
Be,
We're lonely,
Singing to the open night sky
With the fires listening not too far away.

We left the city to grow up on this grass,
Me and
He who brings me poetry
Lets me stay awhile,
Suddenly it's eternity
And if the flames were to take us
We wouldn't mind dying here.

PRETTY

My boyfriend belongs to the pretty people –
With beach hair
glossy lips and flattering clothes
cheeks of perfect blush –
     Those people.

People don't know who I am, who we are
Sometimes we seem estranged
And oftentimes I'm found in the corner of the bar
while he's off playing tricks in the stars,
Until he returns to earth, staying just long enough
to wrap me up from behind
gently rocking me for anchorage.
He tends to float off
     hypnotically
wherever the moonbeams of the pretty people go.

I pick him up in my practical white Kia
pretending it's the classic Cadillac we want
     – In any colour –
I laughingly can't afford,
And he thinks I'm crazy
but lets me wear him anyway
and dress him in the latest New York Fall,
Hanging off his tinted glasses
in attempts to belong to the pretty people.

I don't know what he's doing with me
I'm sure he's not sure either
I'm always on the outskirts of his circle
one step off in his mockery line dance;
     He looks so cool,
unfazed in every line of flattery

While I silently stare and fear my wit
in front of all the friendly pretty people.

But we have the silent things
He lives by the candles and incense and house plants
I,
    by the cool of the moon
and his fingers over my twisted back.
I love that he knows he's the only thing stupider than me
and to strangers I can be cold and intimidating,
Yet he brings out my warmth and clings to it
falling in love when I laugh,
But I will never be one with the pretty people
and he will never dwell long on me.

Cowboy Blues

I'm dancing
With my cowboy
Romancing
Trying to be finer
With the Wang Wang Blues.
Though he's blue
He's got no bang
No rhythm, nor jive
And I can't keep in time
With any clap
Or snap
Of his.
He always has to be on
But he's never on beat
With his Wang Wang Blues
Painted cowboy shoes.

But I keep on dancing
With my cowboy
Romancing
Trying things slowly
Moving like we're floating.
A soft waltz
The only
Thing he knows,
To spin me timely
To surprise me,
Feeling half alive
Submerged in invisible night.
Where finally
He breaks to choose
Me, and he's free
Taking off the cowboy shoes.

THE RAPTURE

As though you were ripped from
the sweet grotto
between the jaw and the collarbone,
I bow my head to the side
Touching cheek to shoulder
as if I were the Madonna,
mourning the soul which once lived
in that sacred space.

Eyes well to the remembrance of your shoulders
Strong and purposeful.
To your enrapturing arms
stirring and seizing
cradling my melancholy,
where they belonged:
under the curated dome of friendship
Transparent seemingly
only to strangers with psychic tendencies.

Intimate looks unknowingly divulge
thoughts of the heart
And you tore them out
with every departure of your eyes from mine.
If it weren't for the folding of your body
around my own
Leading us in a soft rock,
or taking my hand to kiss
like an innocent devotee,
and every other gentle display of yours,
I would say you didn't love me.
But be it despondency or desperation, I'm sure
for a moment you did.

SURELY YOU KNOW YOUR NAME BLEEDS FROM MY PEN

Childlike,
You leaped through my space
With ease,
As I had done with yours
When we'd lay and watch snippets of old movies
And you'd sneak them in my bag to take home.
You drew your name
Onto my blanket
Tracing my own next to it
With your finger,
And I felt I belonged to you;
I tried not to cry.
You remembered to forget and leave your jumper
So I had something to keep me
While you couldn't,
It laid folded, safe.
Such people who don't act on love
Though they are so in love
Are the true romantics,
Cowardly and miserable
So they have art to sell.

THE WIFE

If I was your wife, I would never be seen again

My shelter would become your arms
And I would burrow a home within your body of warmth
Pulling out all which has smashed your soul
Stitching it with my breath

And my breath would furnace your voice
Giving you such a roar, as you had given me.

Our hours would melt into the years
As our bodies kept, mooning over each other
Lying crescent as one.

My people would smell me on you
And wonder where I am

For they are blind
To my entrance into you,
To the depths
The pressures
The tender interlocking of our souls;
You drink from my scent
Thus it radiates from you

Just as the sun's worshipping flowers
Bathe in her oils

You, succulent
From my waters
And fed full of my natural light,
Too, now never removed.

As your wife
I would rock you in my shell
And particles of your being
Would live with every other treasured tone
I've dug through to mould around,
Inescapable.

You would write hungrily on my mind
Of everything within you
So I would walk bearing your life as my own
And your people would know my devotion

We would scar each other
As evidence of perpetuity
For we know there is no pleasure
If we cannot agree to withstand pain.

I would commit myself as your oxygen
And you would long for nothing,

But my whispers
Knowing they are of truth and gratitude,
And my eyes
Which stand to peel your skin off from its frame
And bury my own body beneath it.

Then,
Returning
Enveloping me in your blankets,
You would know no other
Who could desire your spirit more
Than I, as your wife.

The Occupation

Were they born too late
For the people of this world?

In the art gallery
Schoolboy softly
Tracks down her spine

Knowing to retrace,
Reversing up all lines of safety,
Before getting too familiar, like
The forehead he kisses which rests
On his shoulder. Or the hand
He took as greetings

She forgets when he moved from there
To her cheek, but she wouldn't
Mind if he conquered all these things
Every time, and stayed there, such
As a schoolgirl dreams.

And with that passing,
Leaks out of her
The anguish of dusty
Mirrors and social masks;
Melting porcelain.

The names they gave each other
In their play
Mean nothing now, words
Lost to the air. They stand
Looking at photographs of war

Thinking of how tense
Between them
The air always was in the presence
Of their mind wars over physical affection.
As their bodies move without
Asking, drawn into a homely position.

May the children always be
Positioned this way.

Were they born too late
Or on time for each other?

THE BOOKSTORE MUSE

Where Sappho sleeps
among the dusty sheets
of music, by creaky stairs

you listen,
eyes and ears bending
perchance to catch the call of perfect pages.

Where strangers move like spirits
bound to a floating body;
aimless wanderers of forgotten words.

I study the almond eyes
studying foreign books
as though they mean something to you

you, belonging to the group
of boys who catch my kisses
and hug them to their breast pocket,

writing my name
by the pressed chrysanthemums
in their leather-bound journals which smell of vintage
    deterioration.

In your absence, I've had to kill you off
to escape these pangs
of where the heart is.

Yet, just as I decide to live
away from the tilt
of your knowing crooked grin

does providence bid you write me of this shared dream –
Light reading by the green observatory
post meridian

scrolling
through the antiques you live by
which I could never buy

from the tainting of another life,
despite admirations
of their designs

beckoning.
Fixing the perfect cocktail head spin
of uncanny timing and love language,

I return to stumbling
over the cobbled alleyway,
where I am reached by you

through notes and notes of great love letters
by dead poets, for us
which we substitute for our own

in an effort not to end
every line with: and also,
I miss you.

and
also,
I love you.

FRED

My baby grows out his hair
Shaggy,
My fingers love to live there.

The soft ends cup over
The thick of his turtleneck,
Where I reside,
When he leaps off to lightning dance
In his moody French ways,
To smoke fumes
And scratched grey paint,
To fixate on tragedies.
He's so, so dark in his angst and depression
And I am so in love.

His thunder nights are starless;
Candles light
His Fauvist works
Of distortions and flat colour,
Living only by the breath
Of his existential words.
And I have impressed myself upon him
And he has impressed me upon them.

Fred is changing for me
Without me.

His mood swings are poisonous
They stain me with red
By the bottle
In his vibrant flashes of fear.

Yet I am invisible when he's not looking at me
My whole life is in his gaze,
Where, up-close, belong the eyes of a boy.
He doesn't know I know when he's watching me,
That it is the only time I wake
During his rainstorm's lullaby.

My future has no view
I sing into the emptiness,
The hollow search for purpose.
In the grooves of philosophy
We adapt silently
Synchronised in loneliness.

But, my baby grows out his hair
Shaggy
And I'm happy.

A Ballad for Bud

Bud sat me down in the corner
You don't always have to be strong
Cried in his arms
He settled down fears
I'm here, you don't have to worry

I followed the lines of his ripped up black sweater
And the scar on the back of his head
And when he got heated and mad with the world
I said, *Bud, you know, things will get better*

I watched him run ladders and scream on the streets
I fell in love with his dreams
He leaned into me as we dazed across seats
I think he fell in love with ideas of me

Bud walked me down to the station
Many things said in the silence
Alone in the basement, cried on my shoulder
Thinking he'd never be enough
He may be the only kid I'll ever love

V

Find Me in Claude's Broken Colour

Isn't it obvious
That all I want is to disappear?
Perhaps to the green canyons,
Or the twisted rivers
Where I bathe in the Monet summer
By the bank and scattered patches of wildflowers
I feel I come from.

Still, you push me into frame.
I know it's beautiful after you move me
Into fear and discovery
On the darkened platform where I explode
Away from the simplicity of the whistling nature
I find is within me,

But it's also beautiful here too,
With the glistening air for company
And where it's okay to be alone.

Or on the road often travelled
At the back of my mind
In the passenger seat of my life,
Floating through possibilities
Based on the nostalgia you've left me
And where I fall through to comfort.

And I know I shouldn't always resume here
But it's so peaceful
In my delusions, where I pretend
Not to know how all these things probably won't work out,
Or even perhaps that I don't want them to

Honestly,
I'm not even sure I want to be here anymore.
Just keep painting me this way
And maybe I will become
Whatever it is you think I should,
Connected to one thing or another

Anyone's Impressionism of me is flattering.
I suppose,
With always feeling so far away from everybody
It's just nice to be thought of.

Kiss (in) Summer, Before You Die and Grow Up

The children picnic along the bank
Glassy waters shimmer
The tyre gently swinging
They crash their fears away
Breaking the still river,
It's a serene postmeridian.
There are baskets and blankets
And clothes on the grass,
Cars parked not too far
The dirt trail walk to the ravine
Is guarded by pine trees
And smaller woodland shrubbery.
This small oasis
Secluded from the trivial worries of town
Neglects inevitable responsibilities,
They come here to feel alive again.
They graze around with laughter
Carefree and glowing,
Cow Parsley in hair
Woven in chains,
The only thing left
Connecting them
Until they, one day, return.
Later on, into the starry night
Smells of berry pie still linger
Whiffs of smokes from fires far away
Drift into their valley,
Here the children lie dreaming
Along the banks of the river.
They'll always be nostalgic
For this heat of the summer
When friendships had more meaning
And their touch with nature was cosmic.

A *POEM* POEM

By the black lake I play
I lay in the shaded sun
roll down the steep hill

Crabs claw at life in the boiling pot
She cackles.
Cracked eggs
chocolate flakes on linoleum
Freddy drifts on by
He does not belong to us
but we greet him as though he does
I long to see him fly

Like the kookaburras,
Or the pecking
wake-up call against the glass

Time does not live here
and nobody gets hurt
the news talks of things happening far away
She runs down the street after Mr. Whippy
for us
There is no wasted day

I have the stones in my cabinet for scent
My finger runs over the scar
left there by sharp cement
humbling me
never will I run walls again

I wonder where my bike is,
or if it remembers me
and the songs I would sing?

Does my sweat and spirit still linger in the grooves of the
     handle bar?
I pray it's not alone somewhere
Dismantled
in some junk yard

Do the trees still feel my gaze?
Are bits of my skin embedded within the bark, just as the
     splinters tried with me?

Does the water recall my feet
where I first paddled?
Can it still taste my lips, saliva, from when I coughed it up?

Does the land long for me?
As a sister knows a sister,
Does the salt of the lake hear the call of my tears yearning to
     reunite?

I am afraid,
That in truth, when they sold you
they sold my childhood.
Maybe one day
when the kids have grown up
we'll return to you,
My sweet, little lake.

children with baskets woven of forget-me-nots / falling like hairs on the fine grass / strands / threads of speech / interjecting observations / attention spanning only the beautiful / effervescent air / soft pillow clouds / blotted paint / pierced streams of shine / bouncing ribbons in rhythm to their pastime / singing forget me not to the spring //

And once this dusky space has cleared,
Flower wreaths belonging to girls
Amongst curls and ivory dresses,
Blushing cheeks
And pearl garden garlands
Dancing in the spring.
Cheese and fruits, like grape vines
Along checkered blankets
Laid out candles
As they wait for siesta,
Children's laughter flying off with the air
And they paint it
Light bright winds lifting bride veils,
The soft closure of their eyes.
Now they rest
Their budding life slows down
As misty spheres float around them
Pulling the nightly shades to the ground,
And the oak trees which before had swinging
Tires hanging from the branches
Now shade them in their slumber,
It's quiet with the angels.

THE ASTRONOMER

He watches the constellations
Lined along her body
Marked from the linen of sleep
And he knows her skin has been touched by the world

In this moment
He does not care about her name
Or her body's tumultuous rhythm,
He lives in it
In her recessed atlas
In each subconscious suspension of breath
Every release, a siren to him

He plays with the freckles on her arm
Joining words of devotion with them
Moving to her back, in awe
Fingertips scrolling, discovering countries
On her landscape
His very own canvas
Holding a galaxy
Left to his own devices
And he feels he is the artist

Lips pressing tenderly against her shoulder blade
Signing a work he longs to own
Though he knows it has never, will never
Belong to him
Art, marked by the world
To pleasure patrons of the world,

And before she wakes
And her body disappears
Her soul, he tries to hold

An astronomer's game with the stars
Eternally failing
Lost with the morning light
Unnamed and unknown

As the Water...

You fall into my dreams
Playfully
Carrying me down
The Utrecht Canals
Cleansed
Empress leaves
Of strong green Spring
Grazing over me
And my winged eyes
I fly

Anja
I fall for your lies
Blissfully
Your tongue sings
Of summertime
Your voice plays
The harp of my heart
And I drift
As the patrons on the bank
Fare me well

Like mother
You kiss me
With honey and maple
To slow me on the stream
So you may chant me melodies
For the lute and lyre
I shall dance
Gracefully maidenly
As I whisper to the angels
Which surround you

Fables
Of power and peace
You call to me
All knowingly
Guarded by fallen flowers
Dressing me with wreaths
I suckle on citrus
Simmering on the gloss of the water
In my white paper weight lace
I'm not ready to grow older

Komorebi

I need to go back to where I came from,
I'm finding it's getting cold.
I remember vaguely
I was there for a minute –
a fantasia Spring
a ballad of Keats
nectars and woods and lakes –
It aches:
Professing one's love for the lost,
pathetic and lonely.

Memory,
Tell me
are you timing it,
so we'll both meet at the exit
and reunite?
Goodbye.
I think I'm going home,
But you walk off
into the mist and rain
each minute farther
I'm losing my way.

I dream I'm returning;
Are you taking me there,
To the brief life of enlightenment
where the nymphs come calling?
I remember vaguely
before travelling through this night lit city,
Of wedding the light beams
by the moss stones
And a rhythmic siesta sleep,
while my jars of milk
kept cool in the stream.

Such a kidnapping of my soul;
Now strapped to the iron towers of grief
from the IV of materiality.

I need to go back to where I came from
I'm so cold.
Chromatic visions return to me,
How my heart lives
off the sun which filters through the trees,
I only had it for a minute.
Instead of teasing from the shaded views of consciousness,
meet me at the exit,
Prove this wasn't just some dream land
and suffocate my breath,
It aches.

Wisteria

May you always be as beautiful as wisteria in autumn
Never dormant like my winter
Or as alluring as the vixen bud in spring.

May you always climb to your rightful place and stay there,
Along the stained glass
Above windows of an old country home
Thatched cottages, of oil lamps and original gas fixtures.
Never forgetting your truthful browns

You're a liar
When you invite innocence to touch the vibrancy of purples
Your seeds are poison,
Hysteria.

May I always love you
And caress you
Your sweet smell
Mad as mine.
Madly tranquil entrance of Eden

May I always grow along the vines with you
Romantic scenery, sweeping
Weeping to be adorned
To be eaten in toxicity,
Wisteria.

CAMILLE

Bathing beauty
Under the crab-apple tree
Petals leaving a pale pink layering
Covering sentiments
From hidden lovers

Laughing
Running from the bees
In a white dress
And boater hat
Ribbon flowing to her knees
Youth plays spring in the garden

Bathing beauty
Hanging from the olive tree
Whistling her song of freedom
Feet dangling
Soft grazing the tips of the rye grass
And playing
With the thoughts of tomorrow

Sleeping
Gently to sounds of guitar strings
And lullaby winds
Of beaus and their stumbling chords
With daisies behind their ears
Smiling melodically
Almost melancholy
To their country song of Eden

Poplars

Oftentimes I lay here
Blank and serene
On the side of the fork in the road
Quiet under the lining poplar trees

Thinking of the little girl shell
And paranoia walls of steel,
Deep flowers bloomed slowly
Noticed only when I hadn't been seen in a while,
While my heart escaped to the poplar trees.

And while I'm here
Mulling over my return
To questions:
Why didn't the adults in my life protect me
From the world
And from myself
My self-doubt and distrust.

I'm taken aback;
My bear hug boy friend protected my fragility
Stress melting off to the sea,
Though people touched me
Against me
They couldn't touch my soul

I was invincible
Because he had me.
Though I trusted nothing,
I put my faith in what he said I could be
In my individual strength and fragility

And he had me
Cradled in his archer's bow
Rising for an anchor point kiss of luck
Ready to fly me through the poplar trees
Or to the sky with my dreams,
And I'd succeed with his beliefs
And power shots,
Ready to pick me up again if we missed.
I could be anything

Because he had me
Because he believed in my goodness
Even when I was nothing, alone
Hiding serene
By the poplar trees.

My Arboretum

I fall back on my elbows
With a sun worn face
And watch you dance hazily
To the summer wind
Playfully for me,
From the grass
Of my Arboretum.

I fall back lying flat
With my face to the sky
And draw lines from each skyscraper tree
To make glass pictures
Towering over me,
From the grass
Of my Arboretum.

I fall back into sleep
With my melted face peacefully
And hear the songs of your soul:
To know you are loved
Is to know you have the world on your side,
From the grass
Of my Arboretum.

Don't come for me, I'm flying

Don't come for me, I'm flying
In the ether
where communication is settled
and lost,
White noise
of the Swiss Alps
the snow-capped mountains
And the sun
glazing over the glade
the brooks.
Your spirit by me
only until I send you away
once completion ceases to need you

Don't search for me, I'm hiding
You won't hear me where I am
where I'm going
You won't need me either.
Play on
with your chalks and building blocks
stacked shelves of misery
to pluck from in creative boredom,
I'm over it.
Cut the music
and the talk
The land is singing
and I soar with her

Don't call for me, I'm laying
Sifted gently into the heath
with my grandparents
who raised me

even without the answers,
Along grass hills
gravel ways
and blue skies
I'm fine wherever they are
Swinging beneath great architecture.
I'm beginning to think there's nothing
after this
Nothing is promised,
So make this my heaven
and leave me to it -
The soft air
the breeze,
It will hurt less.

Late Spring

Let us sit in harmony
Full and fresh
Atop blankets and pillows
And all comfortable things,
Listening to soft winds on vinyl
With the afternoon orange glaring
To thermal our arms
From the window breeze
By our plants
And cups of tea.
I read you excerpts of Ondaatje
And you translate French poetry
From old low budget movies,
Holding silence for such beauties
We could only dream to create,
But dissipate in the physical feeling
Of the transcending way
We lay, we lay
Brushing sentimentally
Our fingers on our arms
Before we turn the page
In our ode to these
Simple, peaceful, happy days.

THE SERVANT

I am a lonely writer
I have my tools and my memories
And the imagination of my memories
That is all.
I slouch when I sit
In the swinging chair on my porch
My hair is streaked with grey.
I've grown accustomed
To the humming sound
Of spring afternoons
And the children riding past.
I have my books
My records and my plants,
There are gardenias and geraniums in baskets
Hanging from the tin awning,
I pick apples from the tree
Overflowing into my garden;
I sit out there with old boxes of albums
And trinkets and snippets of joy.

I am a lonely writer
All my quiet lovers long moved on
I think often of how my friends' lives have been
Knowing they think of me not.
I bake pies in the morning
And walk my companion
Most nights watching comfort movies.
I've hung warm yellow bulbs
Across my backyard
They remind me of my youth,
Every Saturday night
You can find me dancing
To slow tunes of poetical truths.

Under the stars you can see in my town,
I hear the shore across the block
Almost touch the lighthouse;
Salt streams like light through my windows,
Memories of the ones I've loved singing me to sleep
I'll die in my paradise, not lonely, not lost.

115

Acknowledgements

Thank you, reader, for holding this book and delving into a little piece of art. I hope it served a purpose.

Thank you, especially, to my family.
Mum and Dad, for the unending support.
Stephanie and Steven, for the pure joy it is to be your big sister.
Teta and Jiddou, for the boundless love.
Opa, for sharing these dreams with me.

Thank you, finally, to the friends who have been the backbone to my eternal love for the world. Those who have read the countless drafts, attended performances, shared poetry with me, and who continuously inspire me - I am yours. Always.